ICAEW
Principles of Taxation

TP06-2121-015

First edition 2008, Fourteenth edition 2020

ISBN 9781 5097 3415 3

British Library Cataloguing-in-Publication Data
A catalogue record for this book is available from the
British Library

Published by

BPP Learning Media Ltd
BPP House, Aldine Place
142-144 Uxbridge Road
London W12 8AA

www.bpp.com/learningmedia

Printed in the United Kingdom

The content of this publication is intended to prepare students
for the ICAEW examinations, and should not be used as
professional advice.

Although every effort has been made to ensure that the
contents of this book are correct at the time of going to press,
BPP Learning Media makes no warranty that the information in
this book is accurate or complete and accepts no liability for
any loss or damage suffered by any person acting or refraining
from acting as a result of the material in this book.

ICAEW takes no responsibility for the content of any
supplemental training materials supplied by the Partner in
Learning.

The ICAEW Partner in Learning logo, ACA and ICAEW CFAB
are all registered trademarks of ICAEW and are used under
licence by BPP Learning Media Ltd.

Welcome to BPP Learning Media's **Passcards** for ICAEW **Principles of Taxation**.

- They **save you time**. Important topics are summarised for you.
- They incorporate **diagrams** to kick start your memory.
- They follow the overall **structure** of the ICAEW Study Manual, but BPP Learning Media's ICAEW **Passcards** are not just a condensed book. Each card has been separately designed for clear presentation. Topics are self-contained and can be grasped visually.
- ICAEW **Passcards** are **just the right size** for pockets, briefcases and bags.
- ICAEW **Passcards focus on the exams** you will be facing.

Run through the complete set of **Passcards** as often as you can during your final revision period. The day before the exam, try to go through the **Passcards** again! You will then be well on your way to passing your exams.

Remember to use the information given to you in the tax tables. The tax tables available in the exam are the same as the tax tables provided in the Study Manual. Ensure you are familiar with what is given to you in the exam.

Good luck!

1: Ethics

The topics covered in this chapter are essential knowledge for the whole of your Taxation studies.

They ensure that your advice and communication is appropriate and in keeping with ICAEW's requirements.

Topic List

Fundamental principles

Frameworks

Conflicts of interest

Tax avoidance and tax evasion

Money laundering

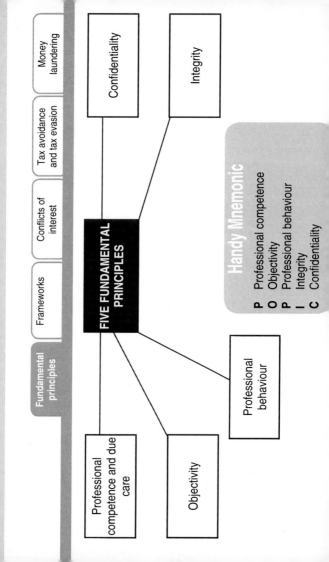

Fundamental principles

| Frameworks | Conflicts of interest | Tax avoidance and tax evasion | Money laundering |

FIVE FUNDAMENTAL PRINCIPLES

- Professional competence and due care
- Objectivity
- Professional behaviour
- Confidentiality
- Integrity

Handy Mnemonic

- **P** Professional competence
- **O** Objectivity
- **P** Professional behaviour
- **I** Integrity
- **C** Confidentiality

1 Integrity

Being straightforward and honest in all professional and business relationships

2 Objectivity

Obligation not to compromise professional or business judgement because of:

- bias;
- conflict of interest; or
- undue influence of others.

Frameworks · Conflicts of interest · Tax avoidance and tax evasion · Money laundering

3 Professional competence

- Attain and maintain professional knowledge and skill
- So a client or employer receives competent professional service
- Based on current developments in practice, legislation and techniques

- Appropriate training and supervision
- Make clear to clients any limitations relating to the service being provided

Due care

Act diligently in accordance with applicable technical and professional standards when providing professional services

4 Confidentiality

Obligation not to **use** or **disclose** confidential information acquired in the course of professional and business relationships, even in a social environment, or to use it to personal advantage or the advantage of third parties

UNLESS:

- You have specific and proper authorisation by the client/employer
- There is a legal or professional right to do so

5 Professional behaviour

- Protect reputation of the profession
- Comply with laws and regulations eg,
  - Anti-money laundering regulations
  - ICAEW Code

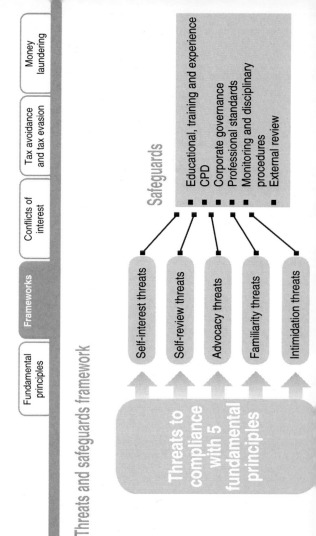

Threats and safeguards framework

| Fundamental principles | Frameworks | Conflicts of interest | Tax avoidance and tax evasion | Money laundering |

Threats to compliance with 5 fundamental principles

- Self-interest threats
- Self-review threats
- Advocacy threats
- Familiarity threats
- Intimidation threats

Safeguards

- Educational, training and experience
- CPD
- Corporate governance
- Professional standards
- Monitoring and disciplinary procedures
- External review

Ethical conflict resolution framework

Consider:

- Relevant facts
- Relevant parties
- Ethical issues involved
- Fundamental principles related to the matter in question
- Established internal procedures
- Alternative courses of action

Seek internal advice if remains unresolved

- Document issue and details

Seek legal or professional advice if necessary

Last resort: withdraw from team or resign

| Fundamental principles | Frameworks | Conflicts of interest | Tax avoidance and tax evasion | Money laundering |

Take reasonable steps to avoid, identify and resolve conflicts of interest.

Conflict situations

For example, where a firm acts for both:

- A husband and wife in a divorce settlement
- A company and an employee being made redundant

Test:

Would a reasonable and informed observer perceive that objectivity is likely to be impaired?

Threats

- **Evaluate threats:** Business interests or relationships with client or third party that could give rise to threats?

- **Apply safeguards:** eg, notify all known relevant parties of the conflict

Alert! Do not act if one of the five fundamental principles is unacceptably threatened.

Tax avoidance

- Legal method of reducing taxpayer's liability
- Can include exploiting legal 'loopholes'
- However, steps taken to minimise tax may not be acceptable to HMRC

Dealing with avoidance

- Disclosure of tax avoidance schemes
- Courts can strike down planning schemes with transactions that have no commercial purpose
- HMRC can challenge abusive tax avoidance arrangements using the GAAR

Tax evasion

- Illegal
- Deliberately misleading HMRC eg,
  1. Suppressing information
  2. Providing false information
- Serious cases can lead to criminal prosecution
- May have money laundering implications

Money laundering main offences:

- Penalties:
  - Unlimited fines
  - Up to 14 years' imprisonment

- Conceal, disguise, convert, transfer or remove (from UK) criminal property
- Enter into/involved in an arrangement which know/suspect facilitates the use/control of criminal property
- Acquire, use or have possession of criminal property (including the proceeds of tax evasion)

Related offences

1. Failure to submit a SAR

2. Tipping off a client

- Penalties:
  - Unlimited fines
  - Up to five years' imprisonment

Reports

1. Internal report to Money Laundering Reporting Officer (MLRO)

2. MLRO may submit a suspicious activity report (SAR) to National Crime Agency (NCA)

2: Introduction to taxation

This chapter contains essential background knowledge that underpins the whole of your later studies of taxation.

| Objectives of taxation | Liability to tax | Tax administration | Relevant influences | Sources of tax law and practice |

Economic factors

Taxation represents a withdrawal from the UK economy. Tax policies can be used to encourage and discourage certain types of activity

Encourages

- ☑ Saving
- ☑ Charitable donations
- ☑ Investment in business
- ☑ Entrepreneurs

Relevant influences

- EU, esp VAT
- Bank Levy
- OECD model tax treaty
- Scottish and Welsh taxes

Discourages

- ☒ Smoking
- ☒ Alcohol
- ☒ Motoring

Social factors

Tax policies can be used to redistribute wealth

- Direct taxes – tax only those who have these resources
- Indirect taxes – discourage spending
- Progressive taxes – target those who can afford to pay

Environmental factors

Taxes may be levied for environmental reasons

- Climate change levy
- Landfill tax
- Motor vehicle taxes based on CO_2 emissions

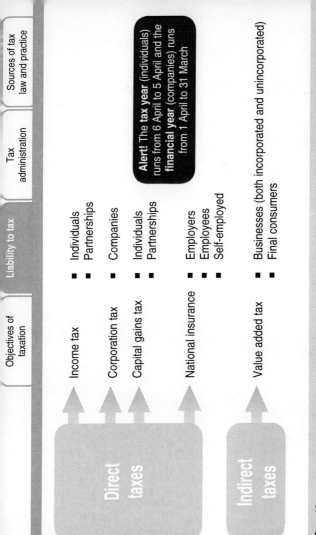

Direct taxes

Income tax →
- Individuals
- Partnerships

Corporation tax →
- Companies

Capital gains tax →
- Individuals
- Partnerships

National insurance →
- Employers
- Employees
- Self-employed

Indirect taxes

Value added tax →
- Businesses (both incorporated and unincorporated)
- Final consumers

Alert! The **tax year** (individuals) runs from 6 April to 5 April and the **financial year** (companies) runs from 1 April to 31 March

Structure of the UK tax system

HMRC

- Collect and administer taxes
- Pay and administer tax credits and child benefit
- Collect student loan repayments
- Ensure minimum wage rules are met
- Protect society from tax fraud

- Commissioners of HMRC
- Officers of Revenue and Customs

Sources of tax law and practice

Law	Practice
■ Statute ■ Statutory instruments ■ Case law	■ HMRC manuals ■ Statements of practice ■ Extra-statutory concessions ■ Press releases and explanatory notes ■ Leaflets

3: Introduction to income tax

The calculation of income tax is key in the Principles of Taxation exam.

This chapter first helps you to identify chargeable and exempt income.

It then deals with the income tax computation, which draws together all of the taxpayer's income.

Topic List

Chargeable and exempt income

Computation of taxable income

Computing tax payable

Allowances for married couples

Types of income

The main types of income for individuals are:

- Income from employment
- Profits of trades
- Property income
- Savings and investment income, including interest and dividends

- Other miscellaneous income

Exempt income

- Interest on NS&I certificates
- Income arising on ISAs and Junior ISAs
- Betting and lottery winnings
- Premium Bond winnings
- Social security benefits (eg, housing benefit)
- Scholarships
- Income tax repayment interest
- Apprenticeship bursaries for care leavers
- Qualifying compensation scheme payments

Leave exempt income out of personal tax computation

Income taxed at source

Employment income – tax deducted under PAYE system

■ given **gross** amount in exam ie, before tax deducted

Income received gross

Received with no tax deducted at source:

- Trading
- Property
- Interest eg, bank interest, NS&I accounts, government securities, loans between friends
- Dividends

Personal allowance

Everybody can deduct the personal allowance of £12,500 (2020/21) in computing their taxable income

- Personal allowance is restricted if net income > £100,000.
- Additional rate taxpayers have no personal allowance.

Completely withdrawn if > £125,000

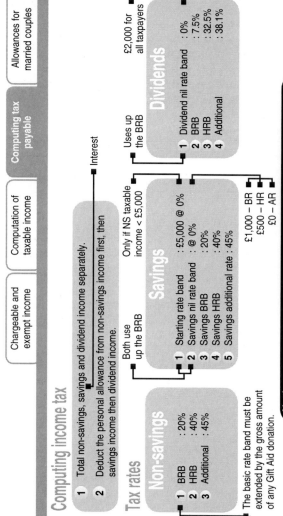

Computing income tax

Chargeable and exempt income	Computation of taxable income	Computing tax payable	Allowances for married couples

Computing income tax

1 Total non-savings, savings and dividend income separately.

2 Deduct the personal allowance from non-savings income first, then savings income then dividend income.

Interest

Tax rates

Non-savings

1 BRB : 20%
2 HRB : 40%
3 Additional : 45%

The basic rate band must be extended by the gross amount of any Gift Aid donation.

Savings

Both use up the BRB

Only if NS taxable income < £5,000

1 Starting rate band : £5,000 @ 0%
2 Savings nil rate band : @ 0%
3 Savings BRB : 20%
4 Savings HRB : 40%
5 Savings additional rate : 45%

£1,000 – BR
£500 – HR
£0 – AR

Dividends

£2,000 for all taxpayers

Uses up the BRB

1 Dividend nil rate band : 0%
2 BRB : 7.5%
3 HRB : 32.5%
4 Additional : 38.1%

Alert!
Reduce liability by tax deducted at source from employment income via PAYE

Marriage allowance

Basic rate TP (or non-TP) can transfer £1,250 of PA to basic rate spouse/civil partner with relief given as 20% **tax reduction**

Must make an election

Personal allowance of claimant spouse unaffected

Not available if either spouse has income in the higher rate band

3: Introduction to income tax

Topic List

Assessable employment income

Taxable benefits

Exempt benefits

Pay As You Earn (PAYE)

You need to know when and how employment income is assessed.

Benefits frequently appear in the exam so it is vital that you are able to calculate the taxable value of benefits provided to employees. You also need to be able to identify those tax efficient benefits that can be provided free of tax.

Employment income is administered through the PAYE system. You must know this area in detail.

Assessable employment income	Taxable benefits	Exempt benefits	Pay As You Earn (PAYE)

Employment income

Employees/directors are taxed on income from their employment:

- Cash earnings
- Benefits

Earnings are taxed in the tax year in which they are received

Date of receipt is the earlier of:

- the time payment is made
- the time entitlement to payment arises

Specific rules for certain benefits

- If specific rule doesn't apply use cost to employer
- Deduct amounts paid by the employee (except for fuel)

Vouchers

- Cash vouchers
- Credit token (eg, credit cards)
- Non-cash vouchers

Cost of providing benefit is taxable.

Living accommodation

Annual value of accommodation is a taxable benefit on all employees, unless job-related.

Additional yearly benefit if costs more than £75,000.

Excess × official rate of interest at the start of the tax year.

Living expenses

Living expenses connected with accommodation (eg, gas bills) are taxable

Private use of asset

Where an asset is made available for private use, 20% of the market value when the asset was first provided is taxable

Use this rule if furniture is provided in accommodation

Cars

- There is no tax charge for use of a pool car.

Annual taxable benefit for private use of a car is:

(list price of the car + optional accessories) x %

- % depends on car's CO_2 emissions
- 0g/km: 0%
- 1-50g/km: 14% unless the car has electric range at least 30 miles (reduced % of 2% to 12%)
- 51g/km to 74g/km: 15% – 19% (increasing by 1% per 5g of CO_2)
- 75g/km: 20% – increases by 1% for each 5g/km up to max of 37%
- Increased by 4% for diesel cars if not RDE2 compliant (max still 37%)
- Reduced by 2% if car registered on/after 6 April 2020
- Scale down benefit on time basis if not available for whole tax year
- Then reduce benefit by any contribution by employee for private use

Vans

- £3,490 for unrestricted private use unless zero emissions when taxable benefit of £2,792
- £666 fuel benefit

Fuel for private use:

- Same % as car benefit x base figure (£24,500 for 2020/21)
- No reduction for partial contribution by employee

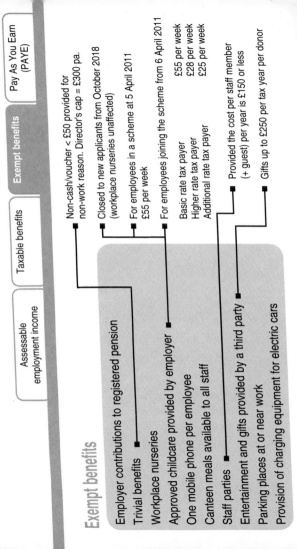

| Assessable employment income | Taxable benefits | Exempt benefits | Pay As You Earn (PAYE) |

Exempt benefits

Employer contributions to registered pension

Trivial benefits — Non-cash/voucher < £50 provided for non-work reason. Director's cap = £300 pa.

Workplace nurseries — Closed to new applicants from October 2018 (workplace nurseries unaffected)

Approved childcare provided by employer —
For employees in a scheme at 5 April 2011
£55 per week

For employees joining the scheme from 6 April 2011
Basic rate tax payer — £55 per week
Higher rate tax payer — £28 per week
Additional rate tax payer — £25 per week

One mobile phone per employee

Canteen meals available to all staff

Staff parties — Provided the cost per staff member (+ guest) per year is £150 or less

Entertainment and gifts provided by a third party — Gifts up to £250 per tax year per donor

Parking places at or near work

Provision of charging equipment for electric cars

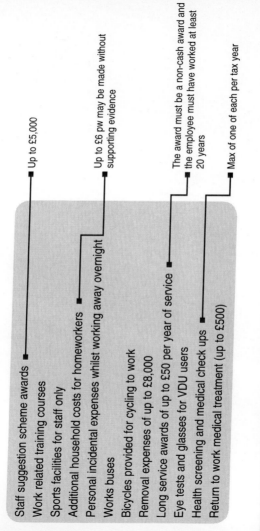

Staff suggestion scheme awards — Up to £5,000

Work related training courses

Sports facilities for staff only

Additional household costs for homeworkers — Up to £6 pw may be made without supporting evidence

Personal incidental expenses whilst working away overnight

Works buses

Bicycles provided for cycling to work

Removal expenses of up to £8,000

Long service awards of up to £50 per year of service — The award must be a non-cash award and the employee must have worked at least 20 years

Eye tests and glasses for VDU users

Health screening and medical check ups

Return to work medical treatment (up to £500) — Max of one of each per tax year

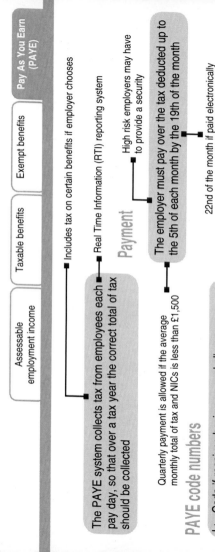

| Assessable employment income | Taxable benefits | Exempt benefits | Pay As You Earn (PAYE) |

Includes tax on certain benefits if employer chooses

Real Time Information (RTI) reporting system

High risk employers may have to provide a security

Payment

The employer must pay over the tax deducted up to the 5th of each month by the 19th of the month

22nd of the month if paid electronically

The PAYE system collects tax from employees each pay day, so that over a tax year the correct total of tax should be collected

Quarterly payment is allowed if the average monthly total of tax and NICs is less than £1,500

PAYE code numbers

L: Code if receives basic personal allowance

M: Code if receives part of spouse's PA (marriage allowance)

N: Code if transfers part of PA to spouse (marriage allowance)

K: Code if deductions exceed allowance

Example

Employee receiving basic personal allowance of £12,500 in 2020/21 will have a PAYE code of:

1250L

5: Trading profits

Topic List

Badges of trade

Allowable and disallowable expenditure

Other adjustments

The 'badges of trade' can be used to determine whether an individual is carrying on a trade. If a trade is being carried on, the profits of the trade are taxable as trading income. Otherwise the profit may be taxable as a capital gain.

In this chapter we will look at the badges of trade and at the adjustments needed in the computation of trading income.

Badges of trade	Allowable and disallowable expenditure	Other adjustments

Handy Mnemonic

F Finance
A Asset nature
N Number of transactions
T Time between transactions
A Acquisition method
S Sale – how carried out
T Trade or interests
I Intention – profit motive
C Changes to asset

If, on applying the badges of trade, HMRC conclude that a trade is being carried on, the profits are taxable as trading income.

To arrive at taxable trading profits, the net accounting profit must be adjusted. We look at this in the rest of this chapter.

Adjustment of profits

Certain items of expenditure are not deductible (ie, not allowable) for trading income purposes and so must be added back to the net accounts profit when computing trading profits. Conversely other items are deductible (ie, allowable).

Allowable expenditure

- Expenditure incurred **wholly and exclusively** for trade purposes
- Gifts to customers costing not more than £50 per donee per year — The gift must carry a conspicuous advertisement for the business and not be food, drink, tobacco or vouchers exchangeable for goods.
- Interest on borrowings for trade purposes

Badges of trade	Allowable and disallowable expenditure	Other adjustments

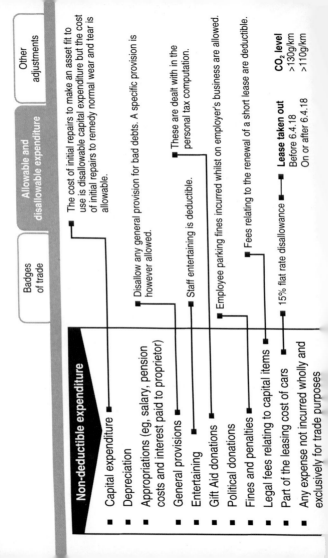

Non-deductible expenditure

- Capital expenditure
- Depreciation
- Appropriations (eg, salary, pension costs and interest paid to proprietor)
- General provisions
- Entertaining
- Gift Aid donations
- Political donations
- Fines and penalties
- Legal fees relating to capital items
- Part of the leasing cost of cars
- Any expense not incurred wholly and exclusively for trade purposes

The cost of initial repairs to make an asset fit to use is disallowable capital expenditure but the cost of initial repairs to remedy normal wear and tear is allowable.

Disallow any general provision for bad debts. A specific provision is however allowed.

These are dealt with in the personal tax computation.

Employee parking fines incurred whilst on employer's business are allowed.

Fees relating to the renewal of a short lease are deductible.

Staff entertaining is deductible.

15% flat rate disallowance

Lease taken out	CO_2 level
Before 6.4.18	>130g/km
On or after 6.4.18	>110g/km

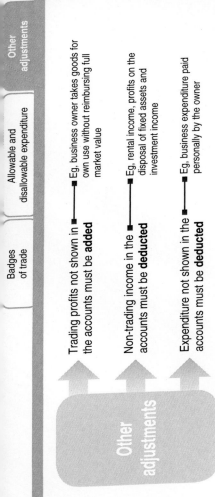

Other adjustments

Trading profits not shown in the accounts must be **added** ← Eg, business owner takes goods for own use without reimbursing full market value

Non-trading income in the accounts must be **deducted** ← Eg, rental income, profits on the disposal of fixed assets and investment income

Expenditure not shown in the accounts must be **deducted** ← Eg, business expenditure paid personally by the owner

Trading allowance

Exemption for trading income receipts of up to £1,000 per tax year. If trading income is more than £1,000 either calculate trading income in usual way or elect to deduct a total of £1,000 (but no other allowable deduction)

Notes

6: Capital allowances

Capital allowances are given instead of depreciation, but they are only available for certain classes of asset. They are a trading expense deducted in arriving at taxable trading profits.

This is an essential topic.

Topic List

Capital allowances

Capital allowances are effectively tax depreciation for certain types of capital expenditure on **plant** and **machinery**

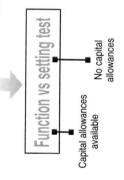

Function vs setting test

- Capital allowances available
- No capital allowances

Plant

- Office furniture
- Equipment
- Computer software qualifies as plant by statute

Machinery

- Machines
- Motor vehicles
- Computers

Main pool

The main pool contains:

- All machinery, fixtures, fittings, equipment
- Vans, forklift trucks, lorries, motorcycles

WDAs

- 18% per annum on a reducing balance basis
- 18% × months/12 in a period that is not 12 months long

First year allowances (FYAs)

- Replace WDAs in period of expenditure
- **Not pro-rated in short/long accounting periods**

100% FYA available for:

- Electric car charging points
- Low emission cars
- Zero emission goods vehicles

Before 1.4.18: CO_2 emissions ≤75g/km
From 1.4.18: CO_2 emissions ≤50g/km

Annual investment allowance

- AIA for all businesses
- Up to £200,000 pa
- Capital expenditure written off in full in year of purchase
- Not applicable to cars
- Max AIA pro-rated where AP not 12 months

Small pools

- Pool ≤ £1,000 after additions and disposals
- Give WDA of full amount of pool

Private use assets

- Keep each asset used privately by the business owner in a separate 'pool'
- Allowances are calculated in full and deducted to calculate TWDV
- BUT can only claim the **business** proportion of allowances

Assets used privately by the owner ie, sole trader/partner NOT an employee

Cars

- CO_2 emissions $\leq$ 110g/km
  - Main pool
    - WDA 18% p.a.
  - No FVA unless new low emissions car (ie, $\leq$ 50g/km)
  - No AIA

Alert!

If used privately by sole trader or partner, put in single asset pool.

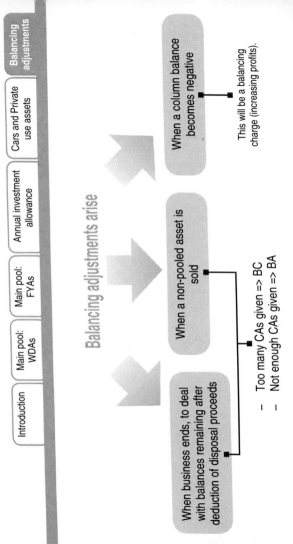

Balancing adjustments arise

When business ends, to deal with balances remaining after deduction of disposal proceeds

When a non-pooled asset is sold

- Too many CAs given => BC
- Not enough CAs given => BA

When a column balance becomes negative

This will be a balancing charge (increasing profits).

7: Trading profits – basis of assessment

We have seen how to calculate the taxable trading profits for a business. We now see how these profits are allocated to tax years.

We also look at how the rules for an individual's business apply similarly to a business partnership.

You must become very familiar with the concepts in this chapter including the cash basis for small businesses.

Topic List

Basis of assessment

Partnerships

Cash basis for small businesses

There are special rules which apply in the opening and closing years of a business.

Current year basis

The basis period for a tax year is normally the period of account ending in the tax year

Opening years

Tax Year	Basis period
1	**Actual basis**: Date of commencement to following 5 April
2	(a) If no period of account ends in year: 6 April to 5 April
	(b) If period of account ending in year is less than 12 months: first 12 months of trading
	(c) Otherwise: 12 months to accounting date ending in year 2
3	12 months to accounting date ending in year 3

Overlap profits

Any profits taxed twice as a result of the opening year rules are **overlap profits**. They are deducted when the business ends

Closing year

- The basis period for the final tax year starts at the end of the basis period for the previous tax year and ends at cessation
- Overlap profits are deducted from the final year's profits

Remember to pro-rate the annual salary/interest if the period is not 12 months long.

Take care if there is a change in the profit-sharing agreement during the period of account.

1 Adjust

Compute trading profits for a partnership as a whole in the same way as you would compute the profits for a sole trader

2 Allocate

Divide trading profits for each period of account between partners. First, allocate salaries and interest on capital to the partners, then share the balance of profits among the partners according to the profit-sharing ratio for the period of account

3 Assess

Each partner is taxed as if they were running their own business, and making profits equal to his or her share of the firm's trading profits for each period of account

Cash basis

- Sole traders
- Partnerships
- NOT companies

Make election by ticking 'cash basis' box on tax return

Join if receipts < £150,000

Leave if receipts > £300,000

Calculating profits

Eg, cash, cheques, card payments or in kind

- Cash receipts **less** allowable business expenses paid
- Include:
  - Capital receipts, eg, on sale of plant and machinery
  - Capital expenditure, eg, on purchase of P&M (not cars or land and buildings)
  - Loan interest payments made up to £500
  - Lease payments on cars (no 15% restriction)
  - No need for special bad debt rules

7: Trading profits – basis of assessment

8: National insurance contributions

National insurance contributions represent a significant cost to taxpayers.

They are a vital element in considering the overall tax position of an individual.

Topic List

Classes of NIC

Class 1 and Class 1A NICs

Class 2 and Class 4 NICs

Classes of NIC

Class 1 and Class 1A NICs	Class 2 and Class 4 NICs

Class 1

Collected on employment earnings under the PAYE system usually on a monthly basis

Class 1A

Collected on benefits annually as part of the PAYE system

Class 2

Collected under the self assessment system

Class 4

Collected from sole traders and partners under the self assessment system with the income tax payable

CLASS 1

Primary

Employees pay contributions of 12% of **earnings** between the primary threshold and the upper earnings limit; 2% on earnings above the upper limit.

For employees under 21 years old and apprentices under 25 years old, only payable on earnings > upper secondary threshold

Secondary

Employers pay contributions of 13.8% on all **earnings** above the secondary threshold.

- Reduced by £4,000 employment allowance (unless single director company with no other employees or prior year secondary NIC at least £100,000)

- The thresholds and the upper earnings limit will be given to you in the exam.

Class 1A

Employers pay contributions of 13.8% on most taxable benefits provided to their employees.

- Generally on same value as calculated for income tax

8: National insurance contributions

The **self-employed** pay Class 2 and Class 4 NICs.

From age 16 to state pension age.

- No contributions are payable if the individual's profit is below the small profits threshold.

- Register once self-employed.

Class 2

Class 2 is calculated at a flat weekly rate.

Class 4

Class 4 NICs are 9% of any profits between the upper and lower profit limits and 2% above the upper profit limit.

- Profits are the tax adjusted profits.

9: Capital gains tax – individuals

It is important that you can calculate chargeable gains realised by individuals and any capital gains tax payable.

Topic List

Chargeable and exempt persons, assets and disposals

Computing CGT

Chattels

Chargeable persons, assets and disposals

Three elements are needed for a chargeable gain to arise.

1. A **chargeable disposal**: this includes sales, gifts and the destruction of assets. Transfer of assets on death is not chargeable.

2. A **chargeable person**: companies and individuals are chargeable persons.

   - Companies are not eligible for the annual exempt amount.

3. A **chargeable asset**: most assets are chargeable, but some assets are exempt.

   - Cash
   - Cars
   - Some chattels (eg, racehorses)
   - Gilts
   - NS&I certificates/premium bonds
   - ISA investments
   - Treasury Stock

Computation

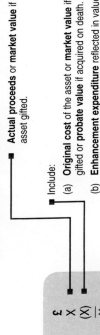

Actual proceeds or **market value** if asset gifted.

Include:

(a) **Original cost** of the asset or **market value** if gifted or **probate value** if acquired on death.

(b) **Enhancement expenditure** reflected in value of the asset at the time of disposal.

(c) **Incidental costs** of **acquisition** and **disposal**.

Annual exempt amount for individuals £12,300 for 2020/21

Tax amount of gains equal to unused basic rate band (£37,500 for 2020/21) at 10%. Tax remaining gains at 20%.

	£
Proceeds	X
Less: Cost	(X)
Chargeable gain	X
Less: Annual exempt amount	(X)
Taxable gain	X
Tax at 10% / 20%	X

| Chargeable and exempt persons, assets and disposals | Computing CGT | Chattels |

Chattels

A chattel is an item of **tangible moveable property** (eg, a painting)

Gains on chattels sold for gross proceeds of £6,000 or less and acquired for £6,000 or less are exempt

The maximum gain on chattels sold for more than £6,000 is ⁵/₃ (gross proceeds − £6,000)

Losses on chattels sold for under £6,000 are restricted by assuming the gross proceeds are £6,000

Wasting chattels

Wasting chattels are exempt from CGT unless capital allowances could have been claimed on them

Wasting: remaining estimated useful life of 50 years or less.
eg, animals, computers, boats.

10: Corporation tax

The profit adjustment rules that we saw earlier for individuals in business apply equally when calculating a company's taxable total profits.

You then need to ensure you use the correct computation rules to calculate the corporation tax.

Topic List

Charge to corporation tax

Taxable total profits

Computation and payment of corporation tax

A UK resident company is subject to corporation tax on its worldwide profits.

Charge to corporation tax	Taxable total profits	Computation and payment of corporation tax

- incorporated in UK
- central management and control in UK

Period of account

A period of account is the period for which accounts are prepared

Accounting period

An accounting period is the period for which corporation tax is charged

- Starts when the company starts to trade, or acquires a source of income or immediately after the end of the previous accounting period.
- Ends 12 months after it starts or, if earlier, when the period of account ends

Alert! An accounting period can never be more than 12 months. If a company prepares accounts for a longer period, that period of account must be split into two corporation tax accounting periods.

First accounting period = first 12 months

Second accounting period = remaining months

Taxable total profits

A company's taxable total profits are arrived at by aggregating its various sources of income and chargeable gains and then deducting qualifying donations

Trading profits

Interest from non-trading loan relationships (eg, bank/building society interest)

Income not otherwise charged

Income from property in the UK

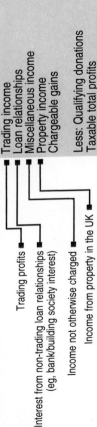

Pro forma for calculating taxable total profits

	£
Trading income	X
Loan relationships	X
Miscellaneous income	X
Property income	X
Chargeable gains	X
	X
Less: Qualifying donations	(X)
Taxable total profits	X

Alert! Exempt dividends from other companies are not included in taxable total profits.

| Charge to corporation tax | Taxable total profits | Computation and payment of corporation tax |

Alert! There is never a disallowance of expenditure or restriction of capital allowances for private use for a company.

Trading income

The computation of trading profits follows income tax principles

Pro forma

	£	£
Net profit per accounts		X
Add expenditure not allowed for tax purposes		
	X	
	X	X
Deduct		
Income not taxable as trading income	X	
Expenditure not charged in the accounts but allowable for tax	X	
Capital allowances	X	(X)
Trading income		X

Property income

Rental income is taxed on an accruals (not receipts) basis

Note. Interest on a loan taken out to buy rental property is deducted under the loan relationship rules (see later), not from the property income.

Dividends

- Ignore exempt dividends when computing taxable total profits
- Consider dividends received when determining CT payment date (see later)

Loan relationships: non trading interest

- Received gross
- Non-trading loan interest payable is deducted from interest receivable to arrive at a profit or loss on loan relationships (see later)

Qualifying charitable donations

- Charitable donations are paid gross
- Deduct amount paid from total income and gains

Company chargeable gains

1. Include in taxable total profits
2. No annual exempt amount
3. Index to the date of disposal of an asset

- Indexation factor is:

$$\frac{\text{RPI for month of disposal} - \text{RPI for month of acquisition}}{\text{RPI for month of acquisition}}$$

- Use Dec 17 if disposal after 2017. Round answer to three decimal places, then multiply by expenditure

Loan relationships

Charge to corporation tax	Taxable total profits	Computation and payment of corporation tax

A company that borrows or invests money has a loan relationship

Trading loan relationship

- Loan for trade purposes (eg, debentures issued to raise money to buy business plant and machinery)
- Costs (eg, interest) accruing are deductible trading income expenses
- Income accruing (eg, interest income) is taxable as trading income (rare)

Non-trading loan relationship

- Held for non-trade purposes (eg, bank account held for investment purposes)
- Income accruing taxed as a loan relationship credit
- Costs accruing (eg, interest on a loan to purchase a let property) are deducted from the interest income

Net deficit (ie, loss) can be relieved

Rate

Rate of corporation tax (CT) is 19% for Financial Year 2020

A financial year runs from 1 April in one year to 31 March in the next. **Financial Year 2020 (FY 2020) runs from 1 April 2020 to 31 March 2021**

Payment date

Depends on level of the company's 'augmented profits'

Taxable total profits plus exempt ABGH distributions

UK and overseas dividends from non-51% subsidiaries

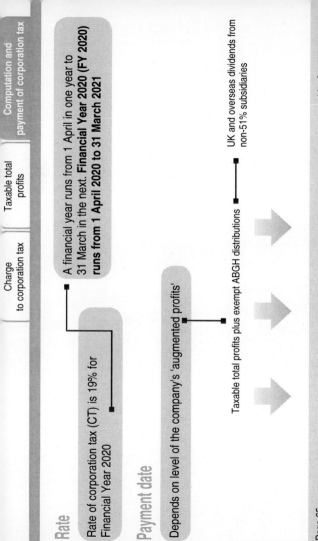

Computation and payment of corporation tax	Taxable total profits	Charge to corporation tax

Augmented profits (AP)

≤ £1.5 million

Payment due date is 9 months and 1 day after the end of the accounting period

> £1.5 million

- Multiply by months/12 for short accounting periods
- Divide by number of **'related 51% group companies'** (plus this co) at the end of the previous accounting period
  - Include 51% subsidiaries (directly or indirectly own >50%)
  - Ignore passive companies

'Large' company so payment due in instalments unless:

- CT liability < £10,000, or
- Not large in PY, and APs ≤ £10 million

- For a 12 month accounting period instalments are due in months 7, 10, 13 and 16 after the start of the accounting period.
- Instalments are due on 14th day of the month

'Very large' companies: augmented profits > £20m in APs starting on/after 1.4.19; instalments are 4 months earlier, ie, months 3, 6, 9 and 12

11: Value added tax

VAT is a tax with many detailed rules.

It is essential to take time to understand VAT.

Topic List

Principles of value added tax (VAT)

Classification of supplies

Registration and deregistration

Output VAT

Input VAT

| Principles of value added tax (VAT) | Classification of supplies | Registration and deregistration | Output VAT | Input VAT |

VAT is a tax on turnover, not on profits. It is imposed at each stage in a chain of sales, in such a way that the burden falls on the final consumer.

VAT applies to **taxable supplies** of goods and services made in the UK by a **taxable person** in the course of a business

A taxable supply is a supply of goods or services made in the UK, other than an exempt supply or supply outside the scope of VAT.

A taxable person is a person that is registered

Supplies

A taxable supply is either standard rated, reduced rate or zero rated

Gift of goods

Normally a supply at cost but business gifts are not supplies if:

- the cost to the donor is £50 or less; or
- the gift is a sample.

1 Standard-rated supplies

Taxable at 20%
All supplies which are not specifically zero-rated, reduced rate or exempt

2 Reduced rate supplies

Taxable at 5%

3 Zero-rated supplies

Taxable at 0%
Can recover input VAT

4 Exempt supplies

Not taxable
Cannot recover input VAT

5 Outside the scope of VAT

Supplies which have no effect for VAT

11: Value added tax

| Principles of value added tax (VAT) | Classification of supplies | Registration and deregistration | Output VAT | Input VAT |

Compulsory registration

Limit is currently **£85,000**

Must register if

1. The value of taxable supplies exceeds the registration limit in any period of up to 12 calendar months; or

2. There are reasonable grounds for believing that the value of taxable supplies will exceed the registration limit in the next 30 days.

Notification required within 30 days of the end of the 12 month period. **Registration** takes effect from the first day after the end of the month following the 12 month period.

Notification required by the end of the 30 day period. **Registration** takes effect from the beginning of that period.

Voluntary registration

☑ Advantage: input VAT can be reclaimed.

A person may request **exemption** from registration if makes only zero-rated supplies.

Voluntary deregistration

Can deregister voluntarily if the value of taxable supplies in the following one year period will not exceed £83,000

VAT is due on all stock and capital assets on which input VAT was claimed (unless output VAT ≤ £1,000)

Value of supply

- The value of a supply is the VAT-exclusive price

  Value + VAT = consideration

The VAT proportion of the consideration is the 'VAT fraction' $= \dfrac{20}{120} = \dfrac{1}{6}$

Example

If total consideration is £240, the VAT proportion is £40 $\left(240 \times \dfrac{1}{6}\right)$

| Principles of value added tax (VAT) | Classification of supplies | Registration and deregistration | **Output VAT** | Input VAT |

Tax point

Each supply is treated as taking place on the tax point

Basic tax point

Date on which goods removed/made available to customer.
Goods on sale or return: earlier of adoption/12 months from removal

Actual tax point

Date invoice issued or payment made if before basic tax point

Alternatively, the invoice date, if invoice issued within 14 days after basic tax point

Deposit payment = separate tax point

Fuel

Based on CO_2 emissions

VAT on:

- Fuel used for business purposes: fully deductible
- Fuel used for private purposes: fully deductible but account for output VAT based on a set scale figure

Where cost of fuel used for private purposes is not fully reimbursed to business

Discounts

Where a discount is offered for prompt payment, VAT is chargeable on the amount actually paid

Bad debt relief

- Claim within four years
- Bad debt must be over six months old
- Debt must be written off in accounts

From when payment is due

TPOG-212-315

Irrecoverable input VAT

Input VAT on the following items cannot be reclaimed:

- Motor cars not wholly used for business purposes
- UK business entertaining
- Non-business items
- Items for which no VAT receipt is held

Pre-registration input VAT

Reclaimable pre-registration VAT is

1. VAT on **goods** bought in the four years prior to registration and still held at the date of registration

2. VAT on **services** supplied in the six months before registration

12: Value added tax – further aspects

Much of the detailed accounting aspects of VAT are not tested in the higher level papers, so it is likely that you will see them in your exam.

Topic List

Accounting for VAT

Small business schemes

VAT records and accounts

| Accounting for VAT | Small business schemes | VAT records and accounts |

VAT period

Traders account for VAT for each VAT period (usually three months).

VAT return (Form VAT 100) for each period.

All businesses must file VAT returns online.

VAT liability below £2.3m

Electronic return and VAT due one month and seven days after end of VAT period

VAT liability over £2.3m ('substantial' traders)

Payments on account

Annual accounting scheme

- Annual taxable turnover must not exceed £1,350,000 (excl VAT)
- Annual VAT return
- Traders can apply to join the scheme as soon as they register for VAT
- Traders either make:
  - nine interim monthly payments each equal to 10% of estimated VAT liability; or
  - three quarterly interim payments each equal to 25% of estimated VAT liability.

Payments starting from end of Month 4

Payments due by end of Months 4, 7 and 10 of the annual accounting year

Advantages

- ☑ Only one VAT return each year so fewer occasions to trigger a penalty.
- ☑ Two months to complete the annual return and make the balancing payment.

Flat rate scheme

- Optional scheme for business with VAT-exclusive taxable turnover up to £150,000.
- Flat rate of VAT applies to total VAT-inclusive turnover.
- Normal VAT invoice issued to VAT-registered customers.

Use the percentage given in your exam.

Advantages

- ☑ Reduction in VAT administration burden
- ☑ Possibly less VAT payable

Cash accounting scheme

- Account for VAT when cash paid/received.
- Annual taxable turnover must not exceed £1,350,000 (excl VAT).
- To join, all VAT returns/payments must be up to date.

Advantages

- ☑ Output VAT only accounted for when payment is received
- ☑ Automatic bad debt relief (no output VAT payable if payment is not received)

Invoices: required details

Should include, eg:

- Tax point
- VAT registration number
- Description of goods and services
- Total VAT chargeable

Simplified invoices may be issued where the invoice is for up to £250 (incl VAT)

Modified invoice may be issued for retail supplies over £250

Making Tax Digital for Business (MTDfB)

From 1.4.19 businesses obliged to maintain records digitally

Records

VAT records must be kept for six years

Records must be kept to support output VAT charged and input VAT claimed

Examples

- Sales invoices
- Till rolls
- Cash book
- Bank statements
- Annual accounts

12: Value added tax – further aspects

Notes

13: Administration of tax

In this chapter we look at the common penalty regime for errors, that applies across several taxes. We then look at the specific administrative requirements for each tax in turn as well as HMRC's powers in connection with tax returns, taxpayers and tax agents.

Topic List

Common penalties

PAYE: RTI

Income tax and CGT

Corporation tax

VAT

Compliance checks and appeals

HMRC powers

BPSS and BPP

| Common penalties | PAYE: RTI | Income tax and CGT | Corporation Tax | VAT | Compliance checks and appeals | HMRC powers | BPSS and BPP |

Penalties for errors

- Penalty based on % of Potential Lost Revenue (PLR)
- Apply if error results in:
  - Understatement of tax liability
  - False/increased loss
  - False/increased repayment

— IT, NI, PAYE, CGT, CT, VAT returns

— 30 days to pay penalty

— Appeals against penalties can be made to First-tier Tribunal

Type of error	Maximum penalty	Minimum penalty	
		Unprompted disclosure	Prompted disclosure
Careless	30%	0%	15%
Deliberate but not concealed	70%	20%	35%
Deliberate and concealed	100%	30%	50%

No penalty if due entirely reasonable care

Penalty for failure to notify

Failures
IT, NI, PAYE, CGT, CT, VAT

- Penalty based on % of Potential Lost Revenue (PLR)

Behaviour	Maximum penalty	Minimum penalty			
		Unprompted Disclosure		Prompted Disclosure	
Deliberate and concealed	100%	30%		50%	
Deliberate but not concealed	70%	20%		35%	
		>12m	<12m	>12m	<12m
Any other case	30%	10%	NIL	20%	10%

No penalty if reasonable excuse

Keeping records

Taxable person must keep 'information' to prepare a complete and correct tax return

Time limits for keeping records:

Corporation Tax – Six years from end of AP

Income Tax and Capital Gains Tax
– Fifth anniversary of 31 January following the tax year concerned (where the taxpayer is in business), or
– First anniversary of 31 January following the tax year, otherwise

VAT – Six years

Failure to keep records could lead to a penalty of £3,000, whatever 'AP

PAYE RTI filing and payment

- Submit employee's pay and deductions details every payday

- Use Full Payment Submission (FPS) form

- Must pay income tax and NIC:

  – Electronically by 22nd of month (compulsory if ≥ 250 employees)

  – Otherwise by 19th of month

Voluntary payrolling and benefits

Employer can choose to collect tax and NIC on the cash equivalent of most benefits through RTI (except accommodation and low-interest loan benefit)

Year end returns

Following the year end the employer must submit

- Form P11D (details of benefits) – by 6 July
- Form P60 (total income, tax and NIC per employee) – by 31 May

Employer must also submit RTI forms:

- FPS – by 19 April
- Earlier year update – if necessary

Penalties

Form P11D

- £300 per late return
- £60 per day if delay continues

FPS

- Monthly penalties dependent on number of employees

Late payment of in-year PAYE

- Related to number of defaults in a tax year

  – Up to 4% for 11th or more

  – Unpaid after 6 or 12 months results in additional penalties of 5%

| Common penalties | PAYE: RTI | Income tax and CGT | Corporation Tax | VAT | Compliance checks and appeals | HMRC powers | BPSS and BPP |

Filing date

The filing due date for filing a tax return **online** is the later of:

(a) **31 January** following the end of the tax year which the return covers.

(b) Three months after the notice to file a return was issued.

The filing date for a **paper return** is the later of:

(i) **31 October** following the tax year

(ii) Three months after a notice to file a return was issued

Some taxpayers only need to submit a short return

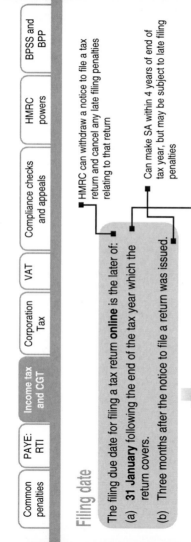

■ HMRC can withdraw a notice to file a tax return and cancel any late filing penalties relating to that return

■ Can make SA within 4 years of end of tax year, but may be subject to late filing penalties

■ If a tax return is not automatically issued, HMRC must be notified by the 5 October following the end of the year, if there is additional tax to pay

HMRC can use simple assessment so no return required

Penalties for late filing of returns

- IT and CGT only

- Immediate £100 penalty

- Daily fixed penalties of £10 per day for up to 90 days if return 3 months late

- > 6 months late, 5% tax-geared penalty — Tax-geared penalties subject to minimum of £300

- > 12 months late:
  - 100% of tax due where withholding of information is deliberate and concealed
  - 70% of tax due where withholding of information is deliberate but not concealed
  - 5% of tax due in other cases

These penalties can be reduced for prompted/unprompted disclosure

Payments on account

Payments on account (POA) of income tax and Class 4 NICs must be made on 31 January in tax year and on the following 31 July

- Each POA is 50% of the prior tax year's income tax and Class 4 NIC liability less tax suffered at source

- POAs are not generally required for employees with no other income sources

Balancing payment

- The final payment of income tax and Class 4 NICs must be paid on 31 January following the tax year.

- Class 2 NICs are also due with the balancing payment.

Capital gains tax

- All CGT is due on 31 January following the tax year

Penalties for late payment

Penalties apply to balancing payment of income tax, CGT or Class 4 NICs:

(a) 30 days after due date   5% of tax unpaid
(b) 6 months after due date   5% of tax unpaid
(c) 12 months after due date   5% of tax unpaid

The penalties are cumulative.

Interest

Interest runs on:

(a) POAs from the normal due dates (31 Jan and 31 July).

(b) Any late final payment and CGT from the due date.

| Common penalties | PAYE: RTI | Income tax and CGT | Corporation Tax | VAT | Compliance checks and appeals | HMRC powers | BPSS and BPP |

Returns

A company must normally submit its CT return within 12 months of the end of the period to which the return relates

Some companies only need to submit a short return

Interest

- Runs between the due date and date paid
- Overpaid tax earns repayment interest from the later of date it is paid and due date – taxable as non trading loan relationship income
- Position is looked at cumulatively after the date for each instalment

Late filing fixed penalties

- £100 ≤ 3m late (£500 if 3rd consecutive late return)
- £200 > 3m late (£1,000 if 3rd consecutive late return)

Tax-geared penalties

- > 18 < 24m – 10% x tax unpaid @ 18m from end of return period
- > 24m – 20% x tax unpaid @ 18m from end of return period

Default surcharge

- 1st late return/payment begins **surcharge period**, then:

Default involving late payment of VAT in the surcharge period	Surcharge as a percentage of the VAT outstanding at the due date
First	2%
Second	5%
Third	10%
Fourth and over	15%

- 2% and 5% surcharges not normally demanded
- Unless surcharge amount due ≥ £400
- For 10% and 15% surcharges, min £30 payable

> Every default extends the surcharge period by 12 months.

VAT errors

Non-deliberate errors up to the error reporting threshold may be corrected on the next VAT return. The threshold is the higher of

- £10,000; or
- 1% of turnover up to a maximum of £50,000.

Alternatively form VAT 652 may be used to report the error.

Penalty under common penalty regime may be imposed.

Interest

Interest is charged on VAT which was or could have been assessed. It runs from when the VAT should have been paid to when it is paid

| Common penalties | PAYE: RTI | Income tax and CGT | Corporation Tax | VAT | Compliance checks and appeals | HMRC powers | BPSS and BPP |

Compliance check

HMRC may conduct an enquiry into an individual's or company's return provided it gives notice by a year after:

(a) The actual filing date.

(b) The 31 January, 30 April, 31 July or 31 October next following the actual delivery date of the return, if filed late.

- Randomly selected
- Identified tax risk

Discovery

Where full disclosure is not made, HMRC may make a discovery assessment. The time limits depend on the reason for loss of tax.

Reasons for loss of tax:

- Not careless/deliberate   4 years
- Careless behaviour   6 years
- Deliberate behaviour   20 years

Appeals

- Most decisions can be appealed
- Time limit: 30 days
- Route of appeal:

Optional internal review
- Appeal within 30 days of this decision if not satisfied

First-tier Tribunal

Upper-tier Tribunal
- Complex cases and appeals from First-tier Tribunal within 56 days

- Request by HMRC to submit documents
- Assessment by HMRC
- Penalty

TP06-211415

| Common penalties | PAYE: RTI | Income tax and CGT | Corporation Tax | VAT | Compliance checks and appeals | HMRC powers | BPSS and BPP |

Information and inspection powers

— IT, NI, PAYE, CGT, CT, VAT

Information notices

- To request information and documents from taxpayers and third parties
- Must be reasonably required
- Cannot request information from tax advisers and auditors

Right of appeal

Inspection notices

- Authorised officer can enter business premises of taxpayer
- Must be reasonably required

No right of appeal

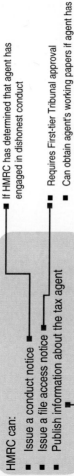

Dishonest conduct by tax agents

HMRC can:

- Issue a conduct notice
  - If HMRC has determined that agent has engaged in dishonest conduct
- Issue a file access notice
  - Requires First-tier Tribunal approval
  - Can obtain agent's working papers if agent has engaged in dishonest conduct
- Publish information about the tax agent

Penalties

- Dishonest conduct: £5,000 – £50,000
  - Only if penalty for dishonest conduct > £5,000
- Failure to comply with file access notice:
  - £300
  - £60 per day

Recovery of debts

HMRC can collect unpaid tax ≥ £1,000 directly from taxpayer's bank account

- Must not reduce bank account below £5,000

Common penalties	PAYE: RTI	Income tax and CGT	Corporation Tax	VAT	Compliance checks and appeals	HMRC powers	BPSS and BPP

Business Payment Support Service

- Helps businesses unable to meet tax payments
- Allows temporary options to spread tax payments over time
- Interest (not penalties) still applies

Budget Payment Plans

- Taxpayer can set up plan to make regular payments in advance

Notes

Notes

Notes

Notes

Notes

Notes

Notes